Sofia Says

By Sofia Degraff

Made with love for her 6th birthday

ISBN:9781533360847
ISBN:1533360847

ii

Introduction

This book was made for Sofia's 6th birthday, so that she would have a record of a few of the wondrously amazing things she said when she was 3, 4 and 5. It's for others to enjoy, because there is so much to think about here, and more than a few smiles to be had. Though I may be just a little biased, I believe these quotes from Sofia comprise one of the greatest books ever written.

-Adam DeGraff

2013

Sofia, born April 20, 2010, is 3 years old.

September 13

Sofia pops her head in the doorway and says

"I'm baby sneaky!"

September 28

This morning we were listening to the record "New Morning" by Bob Dylan and I said to Sofia, "Hey, this record is called "New Morning" and it *IS* a new morning." Sofia said, "Yes! This record knows us. And my sister and I are proud of this record."

November 3

"I can hear my heart beating. That's where the love comes through. That's how the body works."

November 7

Sofia asked me how the tooth fairy knows when we lose a tooth. And how she knows where you live. I told her it was magic. She asked what magic was. I told her it was a mystery. She said,"So Huckle on 'Busytown' is trying to solve magic?"

November 19

"Dada do you want to know what a secret is?"

"Yes!"

"Your beard is way smaller than Santa's."

November 21

"Dada, you live in the sun.
I swam in your eye."

December 1

Sofia's Christmas List:

"I want a kid record player, a record that plays
'Have you ever seen a mystery?,' one of those
things that shoot candy out, a small framed
picture of a really small baby, cat slippers, a new
guitar that doesn't ever get broken and a jack-a-
lantern that lights up.

December 8

"Sofia, I have a mystery for you. Have you seen Lucia's rabbit?"

Sofia says, "I have a better mystery. *I'm trying to figure out how flowers grow in the sun.*"

2014

January 2

Sofia asked me to listen and then sang a song about her hands being dry and itchy that went, "dry dry dry dry dry dry dry dry dry DRY DRY DRY!." By the end of the song she had raised her voice to a scream. I told her I liked the song up until the end. She asked why and I said because it got a little too loud for my ears. She defended her choice by saying, "*That's because it had to die.*"

January 3

Sofia was excited to perform a song for her grandparents and cousins, but when it came time to do it she became shy and froze.

Later as she was going to bed I told her a bed time story about a little plane that was flying just fine by itself, but when it came time to fly in front of the big planes the little plane became shy and froze and then began to nose-dive down to the ground. The other planes quickly flew down underneath her and caught her just in time. They lifted her back up to the heavens on their backs. Once she was ready to fly on her own again they let her go. She flew and was so happy to be flying again she did a loop de loop. All the planes applauded and were proud. The end.

Sofia asked me to tell her another story, a super awesome one this time.

Wasn't that one super awesome enough?

She said, "Yeahhh…but tell me a really really super awesome one.

Okay!

So I told her the story of the blue guitar that loved to play for big crowds, but felt lonely up on stage by herself. The blue guitar went and looked for a friend to play with. She found a red drum just hanging out on the corner and playing by herself. She listened and liked what she heard.

She said, in guitar language, bwa bwa bwa. Translation: do you want to play some music with me?

The drum said, bap bap a boom bop a bippipity boppity boom. Translation: I've been hoping somebody would ask me that all day.

So they played music together and had fun. Pretty soon some people heard them play and came over to watch. A little girl in the crowd named Sofia asked if she could join their group. The guitar said, bwa bwa bwa, and the drum said, bop bap boom! Translation: Yes, we really need a singer!

Sofia sang her big mash up hit, "On the good ship lolli...POP goes the weasel."

The people clapped and were happy. Someone in the crowd shouted what do you call your band?

The red guitar looked at the others and said, "how about The Wa Wa Was."

The blue drum said, "That's good, but I was thinking we should call it The Bee Bim Bops?"

Sofia said, "I love that name too, but I think we should call our band the Yo Yo Yos."

Everybody liked that idea.

Then the band went on a sold-out tour of Europe.

The end.

I asked Sofia if that was a super awesome enough story and she said, "Yeah."

January 6

Sofia climbed on my back this morning and said, "Mama look at me, *I'm the sea of the desert*."

January 9

Poem and title by Sofia as dictated to Dad:

Sofia's Banksy Art

Sofia went on a walk. Sofia knew what to do. Sofia did know what to do, really know, every time she went on a mountain walk. Sofia did not know what to do after she did know what to do on the mountain walk. Sofia knew what to do every time she went on a rainy day mountain walk day. She was a baby, but she still was a big kid. She said yes, no. She went to bed. the next morning she got balloons from the park. Then she smelled beautiful rose flowers. Red, yellow and green. Those were all the colors. She had really good smelling soap. She is going on a walk by herself. She smelled beautiful heart flowers with a stem that was orange. And then her mother didn't hear what she said after she went on a walk by herself after school.

January 10

Sofia says, "*To change your dreams you have to think really hard.*"

January 11

Sofia called the dish I made her tonight, "missile toads." A mash-up pun, somewhere between Mr. toad and missal toe. (Small pieces of yam with two blueberries for eyes and spinach down it's back.)

January 12

A vegan snack called a "soopa" by Sofia. It's a rice cracker with a cube of tomato and cilantro.

January 13

Boiled large yam, cut it in half for monster body. Carrot makes a nose, chocolate chip eyes, cilantro mustache, sausage skirt. Sofia called hers Tootsy Gashi (after her current favorite musician, Kishi Bashi.)

January 15

Sometimes Dada's hand turns into Sarah the Spider.

Sarah the Spider said, "I like to eat little girls."

Sofia suggested vegetables instead.

Sarah asked, "Why's that?"

Sofia said, "Because they give you energy and make your body healthy and strong."

Sarah the Spider said she preferred little girls because they gave her a better sense of humor.

Sofia said Sarah could just ask God for a sense of humor instead.

So Sarah asked God and God said no.

Sarah the Spider said, "Well, that didn't work."

Sofia said try again, so Sarah asked again. But again, God said no.

Sofia asked Sarah to ask God why not, so Sarah asked, "God, why can't I have a better sense of humor?"

God said to Sarah, "Because you are already too funny."

Sofia said, "Ask God if you could get a sense of camera instead."

January 23, 2014

Sofia mash-up song

"Won't you give this dog a bone,
this old man came rolling home,
as you can see."

January 23, 2013

Sofia says, *"I'm stealing all the clocks in the world."*

January 25

Sofia says, "You are going on time out for loving us too much, Mom."

January 28

Sofia gave me an "S" stamp as a gift this morning. I stamped my heart with it. I told her that she gave me a superpower, to be as cool as Sofia. She said, "No, not as cool as Sofia, silly, *as Smart as Sofia.*"

February 1

"Daddy, we really love the world because it's our habitat."

February 3

Sofia told me there was a tattoo inside my ear. I asked her what it said and she replied, "Sofia's Banksy."

February 6

Sofia says, "Santa doesn't live anywhere. That's why he's coming to town. He lives in Space."

February 7

Put honey on corn tortilla. Roll it into a cone shape. Toast until crisp. Take snow from backyard and add to cone. Pour juice over snow for flavor. Sofia calls this a taco snowcone.

February 14

Sofia says, "*There are a million days after a million nights.*"

February 15

This morning Sofia said she was grateful for her name so she could spell herself.

March 7

"My brain is smarter than I am."

March 12

"We're book readers.
We're show watchers.
We're everything doers."

March 9

"My heart is also pretty smart too. But my brain
tells me most things."

March 10

"What is the back of the leaf called?"

March 18

"How deep is the sky?"

March 20

"I'm giving out hearts for patience."

March 27

"I'm warm as fuzz."

March 27

6:46 AM

"Let's pretend this is our house and our door is open forever for anyone to come in."

6:48 AM

"Do you mind closing the door so nobody knows this is a nice person house?"

April 3,

7:50 AM

"The flowers are summering up."

8:31 AM

"Daddy, is laughing happy crying??"

April 6

"Medicine is love."

April 8

"The adults were watching the adult shows like P Town and Mr. Peabod and the giant was a chicken."

April 9

"Unicorns are made of hearts."

(She says she got this idea from her –imaginary-
friend, Baco.)

April 11

As Grandma Bonnie was getting out of the car
she said, "I'm an old woman." After a beat
Sofia said, "I'm a new woman."

April 13

"God says I can wear whatever I want."

April 16

"What are those big bumps on the bottom of trees?"

"I don't know, I think that might be where they store their sap."

"What is sap?"

"That's what trees eat."

"Everybody knows they eat roots, Dad."

April 18

"Did you watch Mickey Mouse as a kid?"

"Yes."

"It seems like everybody has seen it."

April 20, 2014

Sofia turns 4

April 23

"Does God hammer in your heart? Is that what makes the booming sound?"

April 25

"Five minutes? That could take forever!"

April 24

"Dada the sky is dictionary blue."

April 25

Sofia is looking into the mirror and saying, "Dear God, can you please give me too many eyes to see? So many? Thank you, God."

April 26

Sofia says, "We all whine about wine."

Dada: "Like we all scream about ice scream."

Sofia: "We all yell about yellow."

Dada: "Yeah!"

Sofia: "And we read about redness."

April 27

Sofia asks for bread and broth for lunch today.

"Why?"

"Because that's what the lady in the shoe fed her many children."

May 5

"Too much ginger makes your tongue spice out."

May 9

Sofia Joke

"Knock Knock."

"Who's there?"

"Shoe."

"Shoe who?"

"Shoe on your head"

May 11

Sofia was riding on my shoulders today and wanted me to start running, just for fun. I demurred. She said, "Come on, Dad! Run as fast as a 45 year old man can!"

May 17

"I'm an expert kid artist."

May 18

"You have to start telling the truth and not jokes."

May 19

"I love you all the way to *the end of space*."

May 20

"I love you this much" (grabs her hand behind
her back as if to say, all the way around.)

May 21

Sofia says, "I love you more than the end of
Kiki's Delivery service."

May 23

Sofia Poem as dictated to Dada:

Banksy's Side When Going Up The Mountain

One day there was two girls who only sleeped
for one year. And they loved to go on the
mountain side together. And then they loved to
get on a surfboard and swim on the surfboard.
Then they loved to put a lot of chapstick on.
Then they wanted to go out on a river by
ourselves but they couldn't because their mother
said you can't go without us because its really
really really really too far to go without us. Then
they loved loved to get on their surfboards. And
they loved to surf on the same board. Calendula!
Then they loved to go out on the desert by
themselves. Then they loved to lick their tongue.
Then they loved to get on top of owl's back.
Then they love to kiss the bubbles, then they
pop. Then they loved to catch the bubbles and
then they didn't pop. Then they loved to, um,
catch butterflies on their fingers. Then they loved
loved loved loved robot's ears. Because they
find robot's ears. And they're really beautiful.
They drop them on the sidewalk. Every
sidewalk. Then they loved to stomp around while
their sisters are sleeping.

May 25

"What's matter? What's the matter made out of the moon?"

May 27

"There are 500 ways to get to the sun."

May 28

Sofia asks, "Why did the chicken cross the road?"

"Why?"

"Because he didn't know which way to go. Because there wasn't a sign showing the way. And then he got bonked by a car."

She laughs.

May 29

Sofia answers, "*That's because winter interrupted the summer.*"

May 30

Sofia says to her sister, "Come here baby, I have a kiss saved in my mouth for you."

May 30

Sofia says, "I love everybody. Even the people I don't love, I love."

June 1

"I suppose you're the funnest person ever, I mean maybe."

June 2

"That's cooler than blackbird. Cooler than outer space."

June 13

Sofia rides up on her tricycle and announces,
"The heart is connected to the soul."

"Hmm. What is the soul?"

"The soul is the thing that makes us love
everyone and the earth."

June 30

Made up song first thing in morning with Sofia

Dada sings: "I'm so tired in the morning and I'm wide awake at night."

Sofia sings: "I'm going to do something so I don't feel that way anymore."

Dada sings: "I'm going to cuddle with momma because she isn't feeling well."

Sofia sings: "And momma has special powers because she is magic."

July 3

"Hey Dad, can we watch the Olympics?"

"Sure, what sport do you want to watch?"

"Picking flowers."

July 8

Last week a book arrived in the mail from Grandpa David called "How To Teach Your Children Shakespeare." I took its first suggestion in the book and had Sofia and Lucia repeat "I know a bank where the wild thyme blows" over and over again until they had it memorized. The line is from Midsummer Night's Dream. Then I showed them pictures of wild thyme online so they would know what they were talking about. Then yesterday I took them to the High Line in Chelsea. We were walking along and we noticed thyme growing next to the path. I said, "Look girls, this path we are walking down is like a river and there's wild thyme blowing on the banks." Sofia got excited and said, "Grandpa's book has come alive!"

July 9

"Dada, there's a rainbow in your ear, a giant rainbow. *It's too big to pull out.*"

July 10

Mom: "Who pulled the eye off Sparkles?"

Lucia: "It was a pretend monster."

Sofia: "It was YOU, my sister."

July 12

Sofia points to coloring book. "I'm going to call this one rainbowful."

July 12

"Daddy, when I grow up I don't want to be anything. I want to be everything."

July 29

Sofia made a heart stamp out of legos. She asked if I wanted a heart stamp with love inside of it. I said, "Yes, of course." So she stamped my heart.

I said, "Thanks, that was very helpful."

She said, "I do what I can."

July 31

Today Sofia built "the great juice box wall of China" out of legos.

August 1

Sofia points to all the buttons on her outfit today and says, "Dad, I am a business of buttons."

August 12

Sofia says, "I have a secret," and then whispers in my ear, sweetly, "I love you."

I told her, "That was so nice to hear, thank you."

Then she says she has another secret and whispers, "Poop in your mouth and in your eyes."

She set me up.

August 20

I asked Sofia, "Where would you fly if you had wings?"

She said, "*Wherever they needed a super hero*."

August 31

"Dad why do we need to stay on the ground and why do they call it gravity?"

September 4

Sofia is waiting to go to her first day of school, so excited.

She says, "I've got to practice before school."

I said, "What have you got to practice?"

She said, "Not scratching."

I said, "How are you going to practice that?"

She said, "I have to scratch right now and I'm not doing it."

September 4

"How was your first day of school, Sofia?"

"Great! I even forgot about you today, Dad!"

September 5

Sofia and Lucia come in the room with buckets on their heads like helmets. Sofia says, "If we hit each other we have coverment."

September 6

Sofia says, "Dad, how do you translate this into Spanish?" Then she giggled.

(Ha ha. I'll have to check giggle translation.)

September 7

Sofia poem dictated to Dada

Sofia's Banksy Artsy Tartsy

Once upon a time there was slow slow tortoises, slower-than-anything-else tortoises. And then little girls came. And then the tortoises saw the girls and the girls saw the tortoises. Then they became Artsy Tartsies, because they made Artsy Gartsies. And then they found a gray card with yellow and purple on it. Then they thought the yellow would burn them and hurt their eyes because they thought it was the sun. -The End

September 11

Sofia says her ear hurts because she's tired of all she hears in this world.

October 1

Sofia poem dictated to Dada

The Super Power Time of the 13 Blackbirds

The 13 blackbirds ate some magic jumping
beans and each got a special power. The first
blackbird's power is that it can snatch a head off
of you if you're being bad. The second
blackbird's power is it is very fast flying. The
third blackbird could read. The fourth blackbird
could fly in loop de loops. Why the fifth one
could dress up as anything it wanted too. The
sixth one could turn into any shape it wanted,
but it had to stay black. The seventh one could
sleep in a human bed without messing it up. The
eighth one could eat whatever it wanted to, even
human food. The ninth one could blow bubble
gum without popping it with its beak. And the
bubble could last for a long time too. The 10th
blackbird could draw without scribbling. The 11th
blackbird could put its foot in paint and stomp it
on paper. The 12th blackbird could talk. The
13th blackbird could do somersaults. The end.

October 4

Last night I was cutting turnips. I asked Sofia if
she knew which vegetable was hard to turn
down. She immediately, almost before I finished
the sentence, answered, "turn ups."

Then today Sofia asked me what I wanted to
eat. When I hesitated she said, "Do you want
some roll-ups?" When I hesitated again she
started rolling on the floor. She said, "Get it? Roll
ups?"

October 5

Sofia gave me a long thin tower
made out of small Legos and said,
"Here's a piece of candy for
you called a super jumbo forgetter,
because you are always forgetting,
but I have superpowers because *I
am the mother of all mothers*."

October 7

Genevieve is leaving the house for work and Sofia pops her head out the door and yells after her, **"I love you so much *it fills up space*!"**

October 9

Sofia says, "How come mom was so mad?"

I say, "I think she was losing her patience."

Sofia says, "I think she was losing her manners."

November 2

I say to Sofia, "You seem to like all the B music; Beck, Bach, the Beach Boys, the Beatles, Bob Dylan, the Beastie Boys, Kishi Bashi. What about Beethoven? Do you like Beethoven? Sofia raises her arms in the air and says "DA DA DA daaa!"

November 13

"This is my drawing of Humpty Dumpty in a boat being taken by a wave. He is already a little cracked but doesn't know it yet."

November 19

Sofia says, "I am grateful we are not models."

December 1

Sofia, balancing on my shoulders as I write this, says, "I was made to climb up daddies."

December 4

Sofia says, "I love you more than 100 men."

December 11

Sofia says, "I'm the kind of doctor that comes right away when you're sick. If you're into much pain to come to me, I will come to you. I'm that kind of doctor. If you are really really good, you can have the magic fork. Here is a medical book to read. It tells you how to be healthy. I eat three tomatoes and an apple every day to stay healthy. I'm not the kind of doctor to give you a check up, I'm the one that gives you stuff to give yourself a check up at home."

December 17

Sofia says, "You must have a lot of friends in San Francisco."

"Why do you say that?"

"SanFRIENDScisco."

December 19

I put Lucia on top of Sofia and Sofia says, "This is going to be exaborating!"

December 20

Sofia, just stopped to tell me that she did it.

"Did what?"

"*Concentrated on my game until my itch was gone.*"

December 21

Sofia says, "Dada, snapping is clapping with one hand."

(Sofia has solved the ancient zen riddle, "What is the sound of one hand clapping?")

December 26

Sofia says, "I'm going to marry Christmas."

"Oh yeah?"

"Yeah, Christmas will be very handsome and I will be pretty."

"Oh, well, then may you have a happy little new year."

December 28

Sofia joke

"Who let the monkeys in the gates?

"Who?"

"Outerspace."

December 31

Sofia woke up from her nap and said,
"*This wasn't the mask I was supposing.*"
Then she went back to sleep.

2015

January 5

"Can you eat clouds?"

January 7

"Dad, trees hibernate in the winter."

"Really?"

"Yes, they do!"

"Yeah, I suppose they do!"

"*Winter is one big night for the tree and summer is one big day.*"

January 8

"Sofia, you're a natural."

"What does that mean?"

"It means you are part of nature."

"Miss Frizzle and The Magic School Bus must be natural then, because they can go inside of your body."

"Actually Miss Frizzle and The Magic School Bus are fiction."

"What does that mean?"

"That means they are made up."

Sofia laughs. "*Something has to be real for you to make it up. Either that or it has to be words that you string together.*"

January 12

I ask, "Is that true?"

Sofia answers, "*True as Santa.*"

January 14

When putting the girls to bed there's a Hindi prayer for peace I sometimes sing with them. I always ask if there is anyone special that they want to sing the song for. Tonight Sofia said, *"For all the trapped mermaids."*

January 22

"Sofia what do you think of life?"

Sofia says, "Thank you God."

"What do you think God looks like?"

"Arms open and giving sweet nectar."

February 3

Sofia sings, "Christmas is true, if you believe in it. I'm going to marry Christmas, yes I am. Christmas is African, Christmas is from China. Christmas is true."

February 12

Sofia brought me a red bell on a tray and said, "I have a seekless treasure for you under this bell."

"Seekless?"

"Yes, that means *you will never stop seeking it*."

I picked up the red bell and underneath it was a black sea shell.

February 20

Sofia tells me I have two backs. I think about it for a second and realize she is right. I have one in front and one in back.

March 2

Sofia woke up and came in our room near midnight. I took her back to bed and tucked her in again. "What woke you up?" I asked her.

"I couldn't remember the shape of a butterfly's wing," she said.

"That's what woke you up?"

"No."

"Do you remember what did?"

"I was just enjoying the sounds that life was giving me."

"When you were sleeping?"

"No, when I was lying here listening."

Then she fell back asleep.

March 7

Sofia says to Lucia, "I can see you with the eyes on the back of my head, Sis, just so you know."

March 13

Lucia says, "I'm baby bear."

I say, "You are baby bear and I call you boogie-butter. Boogie-butter the baby bear. There's a lot of B's in there I say, a whole hive of B's. Maybe we can get some honey from all those bees?"

Sofia says, "Hey, it's only pollen at this point. We have to wait for the bees to throw up before we can get the honey."

March 20

"I love the sun," I said.

Sofia said "You love the grateful sun, get it?"

I had to think about that one. She was riffing off of The Grateful Dad, which is what she calls The Grateful Dead.

March 22

Sofia says, "I'm watching this whole thing."

"What whole thing?"

"You trying to tell a story. My sister whining. *I'm just watching all of that happen.*"

March 23

Lucia says, "Smell smell go away, come back again some other day."

Sofia says, "Why would you want that? It'll just be there on another day."

April 1

Sofia asks to call Mama at work, so we do and Sofia says, "Mama, there's a giant talking pink pickle in our house!"

"Really? What's it saying?"

"April fools!"

April 3

"I have to sit on some babies. Because I'm a babysitter."

April 20

Sofia turns 5 years old

April 22

Sofia says, "I'm learning to be mysterious."

"What does that mean?"

"*I'm learning to climb things and not cry when I fall and get hurt.*"

April 23

On the plane home yesterday we hit some bad plane turbulence. Sofia said, "This is scary fun!" Then a few minutes later, once the plane settled, she said,

"This scribble I made when the plane was going crazy is now a reflection of the bird."

(I like what my friend Darin Stevenson wrote about this when I posted it on Face Book, "Sages are wise enough to withhold such scorching wisdom from adults. Thankfully no one takes children seriously; for here is a divine vignette of birth, what life is, death, the soul and it's eternities... entire.")

May 4

Sofia says, "Music is the food for something."

"Oh yeah? Food for what?"

"For souls."

May 8

I ask Sofia to get the step stool so she can help
me make lunch. Sofia says, "I'll be right back zip
zip zoom." She comes back a second later with
the stool and says, "It's like I never even left,
right?"

May 14

Sofia says, "I'm gonna sweep up as quick as a
tick."

May 18

Sofia says, "Dad, you're a prisomer."

"Oh yeah? What am I in prisom for?"

"For being so funny."

May 19

I tell Sofia, "When you put your clothes away I will give you some french fries."

"I don't want french fries."

"Even with ketchup?"

"Dad, you know I'm different every day right?"

May 20

Sofia says, "Mom, has anyone ever cracked you up? *And then you got fixed again?*"

June 1

"Dad do you be*lieve* me when I tell you that I love leaves? Get it?"

June 5

"Do you know why Gabriella loves to yell? Because yell is in her name. Get it?"

June 8

"Sofia, are you your own person?"

"Of course, otherwise why would I have my own purse?"

June 12

"What kind of artist do you want to be, Sofia?"

"A food artist."

"A chef?"

"No, someone who makes food prettier. I draw food."

June 13

"Lucia, you are not supposed to take the pickles off the sandwich."

Sofia says, "Yes you are, Dad. That's why out why they're called pickles. You have to pick out the pickles."

June 17

The girls want to watch Pee-wee's Playhouse while they eat lunch. I tell them we should watch something about nature (because by our calendar it is Nature Day) and Sofia says, "But, Daddy, Pee-Wee has lots of nature, like talking flowers and laughing fish. And a pterodactyl!

"Yeah...but those are all fakes," I say.

Lucia perks up, "But Dad, Pee-wee's not fake!"

Foiled again.

June 20

Sofia asked me, "Do you know what's the worst thing a princess can wear?"

"No, what?"

"A tiarable"

July 3

I asked Sofia for a poem. She replied,

Eddy Eddy,
Says he's sweaty
So he went to the Ferris Wheel.

August 1

Lucia says, "We're made out of meat right?"

Sofia says, "We're made out of meat and germs and self."

Teddy O'Sullivan says, "And chemicals."

Sofia says, "I was going to say that but I wasn't sure."

Lucia says, "And giants eat us right?"

Sofia says, "There's no such thing as giants."

Lucia says, "I know, but giants eat people right?"

August 6

I asked for another poem and Sofia replied,

Maybe shmaybe,
I think it's gravy.
Let's go to Old Navy.

August 8

I asked for another poem and, to my utter
amazement, received this,

I succeed
The seed
Of me
In the breeze

August 17

Sofia was standing waist deep in the ocean. The waves were starting to get a little too big, so she raised her palm toward the waves and commanded, "Calm!"

Later I asked, "Did the ocean calm down?" And she said, "Not on my schedule."

September 13

Sofia came into my room and said, "Adam DeGraff?" I looked up and she had a clipboard and said, "Follow me." I followed her into her room and she laid me down on her bed and gave me a check up. After looking me over thoroughly she said, "You have, bee-itus," and then asked me if I wanted strawberry or plum medicine. I said, "Strawberry." She asked me where the bee stung me and I said on my nose. So she poured the strawberry medicine on my nose. Then she took my temperature and told me that it was, "the hottest." I guess I was really sick! She had Lucia, the nurse, go get me some water. Then she gave me a book and told me to rest because I would be sick for a long time.

September 12

"I'm brave like Miyazaki. My bottom feels kind of fluffy."

October 3

I'm in the car with the kids, stopped at a red light. I say, "We're hitting all the lights today."

Sofia says, "*That's because the lights are in love with us today.*"

October 8

Dr. Sofia gives me my prescription.

"You have to make belief friends 68 times a day."

"I have to make belief friends?"

"Yes, to keep you company."

"What about dessert? Can I have dessert?"

"You can have dessert zero times a day."

"I don't get any desserts?"

"Only on special occasions. Like Mardi Gran, Or April Fools Day. Or Columbus day."

"Hey, today's Columbus day! so I get one today?"

"Yes."

Sofia disappears from the bedroom and comes back with a bowl full of granola.

November 27

I say, "The leaf pile looks pretty wet."

Sofia says, "I wouldn't refuse to jump in it. "

2016

January 2

After watching Inside Out, Sofia asks a great question, "*If Joy's inside Riley's head, who's inside Joy's head*?"

January 16

Lucia says, "Who wants cookies?"

I say, "I'll take the butterfly one."

I try one. I tell Lucia it has too much butter in it.

Sofia says, "And it's got a fly in it too."

January 23

Sofia asks, "What if all of us lived in this bathroom, and could only eat what we grew in here?" (Huh. I wonder if that *would* be possible?)

January 28

This morning Sofia wanted to ride on my shoulders as we were walking to school. I said, I don't think so. She said, "Pretty please, *with sports and thunder on top?*" I could hardly refuse her after that.

February 10

Today as we were in the car on our way to Brooklyn Children's Museum Sofia said, "I know what your message is."

I said, "You do? What's my message?"

"*Love your enemy.*"

"Wow, where'd you hear that from?"

"From lots of places."

"So you think that's my message to the world?"

"Yes."

"Well, I do believe that. And I suppose not everybody does."

"I know, that's why it's *your* message."

"How do you know that it's *my* message though?"

"Because I know you."

February 15

Interviewing Sofia

"Sofia, what's your idea of a beautiful home?"

"Covered in vines…and inside there's flowers on the wall…and it's like a whole palace…and it's made out of ice."

"What do you think are some of the most important things in life?"

"Birds."

"Okay, and what do you think is the most important thing you can do in life?"

"Move."

"And if you could move anywhere, where would you move?"

"The end of your chair!"

"The end of *my* chair?"

"Yes."

"And what do you think you will find at the end of my chair?"

"Your back." (laughs)

"And what do you like so much about my back."

"The spots on your back."

"Alright. Can you tell me something about the

universe that I might not know?"

"It looks like The Milky Way."

"And how does The Milky Way look?"

"White and milky."

"Do you think there's any correlation between The Milky Way and actual milk, besides the way it looks?"

"The Milky Way is not in a container."

"Interesting. Now, can you tell me what you want to be when you grow up?"

"An artist and a gardener."

"Thank you, we now conclude this interview."

March 4

Sofia has the idea to write "I like your car" in the snow-covered windshield of a random car as we are walking to school, so we do. I can imagine the feeling of pride the car's owner will have when they find it written there. A little more happiness in the world.

April 4

The girls and I were walking in Flushing Queens and were approached a food vendor handing out samples. We said no thanks and passed it by. Lucia wanted to know why. I told her it was out of solidarity with Sofia, because of her food allergies.

Sofia said, "It's alright, you can have some. I don't need it, I only want it."

April 17

Sofia: "Sometimes when I am laying in the sun with my eyes closed I see music notes swimming through the water like a duck, turning around. And there is flute music playing too."

Me: "It sounds like the music is swimming."

Sofia: "Yeah, through soundwaves."

April 19

Song by Sofia (written herself, without help, by hand.)

"Come and see my eyes. Up in the sky. Love and see my eye. Look up into my eye. Look up into the sky. Covering my eyes. Ho my! Ho my!

Come and see my eyes. Up in the sky. Love and see my eye. Look up in the sky. Covering my eyes. Ho my! Ho my!"

May 20

Sofia handed this to me on the train and said,
"Here, I wrote a poem."

Who are you? I see

you too. Do you

like you? Cook

me!

May 24

I found this poem in Sofia's notebook.

I see a dog. Now

I see fog. All

I see is white.

I can fight with

the white fog. Oh

No! Fighting with the

fog did not work!

Now I can see a little

thing of sun. Wow

now there's no

fog and I see the dog.

May 30

Yesterday Sofia wrote a meditation for me and Lucia:

"Close your eyes and take 10 deep breaths and think about how happy you are. Think about your day. What was your day like? Think about it and close your eyes and listen to the music and you will fall asleep. (Sofia sings.) Okay now open your eyes and remember, meditation is a head replacement."

Happy birthday, Sofia!

May you always be so sweet, funny and wise!

Made in the USA
Middletown, DE
28 April 2019